The S
an

Carol,

Even though you dint know any of these folks, but John They were the salt of the earth. & words cant describe them

The Secrets of the Leaves and Other Stories

Jerry Mills, D.M.D.

VANTAGE PRESS
New York

This is a work of fiction. Any similarity between the names, characters, and places in this book and any persons, living or dead, is purely coincidental.

Cover art and book illustrations by Jerry Mills, D.M.D.

FIRST EDITION

All rights reserved, including the right of reproduction in whole or in part in any form.

Copyright © 2004 by Jerry Mills, D.M.D.

Published by Vantage Press, Inc.
419 Park Ave. South, New York, NY 10016

Manufactured in the United States of America
ISBN: 0-533-14755-7

Library of Congress Catalog Card No.: 2003096893

0 9 8 7 6 5 4 3 2 1

In Memory of Mama and Daddy Mills

Contents

Country Po Porie	1
The Secrets of the Leaves	3
Road Maps for Old Mules, Old Wagons, and Little Boys	31
Old Times Are Not Forgotten Look Away Dixieland	47
Petals and Dew from the Past	49
Whispers	57
Coloil and Watkins Sav	69
The Day the Preacher Came to Dinner	75
The Baker's Dozen	79

The Secrets of the Leaves and Other Stories

Country Po Porie

The setting for many of these stories is in and around the country village of Springhill, Kentucky, in the 1940s. There's nothing very special about the area—nothing to set it apart from any other part of the country—but when you put all the parts together, it's like a dish of po porie (potpourri). The houses are very modest, the churches and stores just standard at best. The folks of that era were probably not harder workers or smarter than any other place, but like all the ingredients in potpourri, their fragrance or blend still wells up in the memories in my mind. Those lives were so much more than I have been able to set down. *Words are so much less than the whole.* There are only a few buildings left and few of the folks and even fewer of their descendants, only stones marking where they rest now.

Dear Son,

    I thought you might be interested in this story about a young boy, who had his life changed long ago. It's about how he made decisions that would affect his life and the lives of his family and their futures. It tells about the four seasons of his life and how he changed his perspective during each season. Young boys 14–16 go through some very trying times when they still want to play with toy soldiers but know they can't anymore. There is a longing to move on but a reluctance to leave the things every young boy loves. This story is about that fifteen-year-old boy and how a river and leaves and an old man open up the world to him. His world will never be the same for him again.

The Secrets of the Leaves

It's the middle of October 1954—a dreary, rainy cold Friday afternoon—as an old white station wagon lumbered down a narrow rock-tarred road, heading west. Jim and the boy were going on the last bass fishing trip for the year. The trip was meant to go to the 11-Point at Riverton, down to the Arkansas line, but at the last minute, Jim decided to go on the upper stretch. The boy knew the river would be high and quick because of all the rain. He had been on the point before to fish for browns and jacks but never on the upper end. Jim had taken him to almost every river in Missouri that you could float or wade. He had become sort of a surrogate dad because the boy and his dad were never close. Jim was very quiet and not a good teacher, but the boy watched and took the good and discarded the bad.

The young lad was very quiet, even for him. He had very little confidence around people due to a speech impediment, lack of social skills, and being raised from a very young age by older grandparents who taught him to "be quiet and you will learn from years of experience." "Silence is golden," his grandad had said many times. This fishing trip was special for the boy, because it got him away from some things he had on his mind. He had asked for some hay for his dog from his grandparents, and there was some reluctance to let him have the hay. This was such a small thing at the time but had grown to be a big problem for him. But his biggest problem was an upperclassman on the ball team who had said something in front of his fellow classmen that had hurt him a great deal. This would stay with him until he was an old man.

As the old car went down on a long grade, he could see the mist and fog that always collects above a river when the weather is cold and rainy. Suddenly there it was—the 11-Point River. It was faster and higher than he had anticipated, and the feeling of excitement was overshadowed by a little fear. A grown man had lost his life on that upper stretch only a week before, his partner barely got out with a broken leg. He had heard all about the mishap at Doniphan, Missouri, where they had picked up supplies and some Otts for the trip.

The river was gin clear when they went across the bridge and was cold and dreary-lookin'. Jim and the boy had not spoken since they were at the grocery at Doniphan, but they both were amazed at how quick the river was at that time of year. Jim started talking and didn't quit for thirty minutes while they set up camp down by the river. The temperature was in the low fifties—just cold enough for a light jumper. When they got all the gear stowed away, it was time to go see an old character named Mr. Huffsteadler. Jim had often spoken about this man and said he was a crotchety old German who had a personality like a "Killer Hun."

There was a winding gravel road up to a most unusual building. One end was on stilts, and the other was pushed up agin' a gravel bank. It served as a boat livery, feed store and grocery, and living quarters for the old man and his wife. When the boy stepped up on the old porch, the smell of supper on the old wood stove met him full in the face. He opened the old screen door that had a big ball of cotton stuck on it to scare flies off. As he entered the store, there was a long plank bench on the north wall, which he immediately sat down on.

The old man came out of a back room, the entrance covered by a kind of see-through, cotton-print feed sack. The sack reminded him of days long ago, and the smell of feed and old scales and all the things associated with his past came into his thoughts, and he became more comfortable with the surroundings.

Mr. Huffsteadler waited on a woman with two little kids. They went over to the meat box and asked for a box of crackers and one-half pound of "balona." The little girl peering out behind her mom's skirt looked long and hard at the boy on the bench and the baby boy with his thumb rammed as far down his mouth as he could get it. Both wore ragged clothes and had no shoes and dirty hair. The boy had seen that look in their eyes many times. It was not only poverty but despair. Their little legs were all scratched up from walking up briar paths. As soon as they got their food, the mom went over to the bench and made them crackers and balona, and they all crammed it down as if they were starved. The boy could feel the old man watching him but gave no acknowledgment. The small family left, and he watched the mom stuff the food in a small poke. They went out of sight while going down a small path beside the store. He would learn later it was the family of a guide on the lower stretch of the river.

Jim started a conversation with Mr. "Huff," and very soon that conversation came to an abrupt stop. Mr. Huff said, "I got no more boats to rent," but Jim was persistent. Every once in a while, the old man would glance over at the boy, who was trying to melt into the old wall. Jim practically got down on his knees and begged for a boat. Just when it looked the worst for them, the old man strolled over to the boy and said, "Come with me." They went down some rickety old stairs and out the back and went under the back of the old building. The boy was wondering to himself just how old was this store when the old man turned and said, "About 123 years." It startled the lad: did he think out loud? *How did he know what I was thinking?*

The old man strolled over to a white, canvas-covered object, jerked one end, and there it was—a new river boat. It was a deep-colored green—twenty-six feet long with just enough rake in the front and rear to get over the most shallow shoal. It was at least a foot narrower than most river boats with flared sides, leaving not much room for error in quick water. It had two live boxes, and the rear came very narrow, which proved a great asset when you entered a narrow shoot and needed that first or last stroke on the opposite side to straighten the front.

The old man said, "I had it built some time ago for me, but things changed." Meaning his arm. It was now just a hook with leather and wire to close the clawlike contraption. "Been setting here for twenty-five or more years. I keep water in it to keep the cypress swelled," he said. "Pick up that end there, son. It will surprise you."

The boy responded and said to his own surprise, "Wow. It's light."

Jim left to get some tomatoes the old man said they could have, and soon as he was gone, the old man said, "Come sit and talk a spell."

Just as soon as he began to speak, the boy knew instantly he was a kind old man. He began to tell story after story about the point and all the changes he had seen. He began to tell about the seasons of his life and how he was about all used up. His eyes were small and the color of milky blue—not cold, as the boy was told, but smart, quick eyes—and he could tell by the old wrinkled face he had spent many a day on that river and missed it even though he saw it every day.

The old man and the boy loaded the long green splinter on an old home-made trailer to haul upstream early next morning.

"Don't let anything happen to her, son. I know I won't get to use it, but it means a lot to me, as you can see."

The boy couldn't help feeling sorry for him, knowing how much the river meant to him and never getting to go on it anymore. Jim came back in a little while and spoke briefly to the old fellow, who had changed back into the old German whom Jim spoke of so often. Jim chatted to the boy on the way back to the camp about how he charmed the old man into renting the boat, but the boy wasn't so sure about that.

"The old asshole came around after all when he saw the money," Jim said.

There was silence on the boy's part.

During suppertime, Jim cut a head of lettuce in half and poured some Otts over it and handed it to the boy who had never had anything like this before. Soon the small steaks were done with the like of sliced tomatoes and fried spuds. It was the best meal he had ever had. There's something about late suppers and rivers. The fall. The sounds of running water. Jim drifted off to sleep after a couple of shots of Jack and water, which left the boy thinking about the events of the day, the old man, the woman and two children. This was like a march back in time. Where time stood still, events were changing—seasons, rain, hot, cold, ice. In other words, nothing changed since Jessie James, the Younger Brothers, and the War Between the States. He knew the old man knew or was told about all this in the past. He wished he could talk again or just sit a spell and listen to him talk about the

Ozarks, browns and jacks, or about what he learned while on the river. He recalled how crisp and to the point was each story the old man told him—almost an urgency in the tone of his voice like he was running out of time. The boy felt a warm feeling when he reflected on the lines in his face, the pale blue eyes, his clothes, his smell. Everything about him seemed like history coming alive. He began to think about the look in the woman's and kids' eyes. He felt sorry for them but began to feel this is where they needed to be. The outside world would be even more painful for them. The boy remembered the Big City and what it had done to him, changing his young heart into a cold, callused body part. But his younger upbringing was beginning to overshadow much of the pain he had endured. He knew all too well the feelings of being alone in a crowd. He thought about his tackle—was everything ready? Jim expected perfect casts and everything to be just right 'cause you don't get too many second chances on the river. This would be imprinted in every fiber of the boy 'cause at that early age he knew he would get few second chances.

    Before dawn, the boy awoke and rustled Jim up. As they scrambled eggs and bacon, the boy noticed the fog and wet feeling was leaving. He could hear the river running in the background more crisp sounding. The air was cold and crisp with the smell of wood smoke and food cooking. You know the feelings you get sometime when something is about to happen and you don't know how or when? Well, the feeling suddenly came over him as he was washing the pots and pans down by the river. Even though he was young, he had had them before and almost every time, something good had come his way. He thought he might catch a big brown or jack or see a deer back there. There had been some sightings of cougar, deer, and bear on the upper point. Little did he know about things he would learn and use the rest of his life.

He was putting the plates and pots and pans back in the sack to be used on the float when he saw the headlights of Mr. Huffsteadler's old pickup. It was an old, used Forest Service truck—green and faded from years of sun, rain, ice, and snow but mostly from the twenty years' beating it had received from southern Missouri roads.

The old man bid the boy good day with a smile and tip of his old hat, but he never acknowledged Jim. Each seemed to know what the other thought about him but was not getting in the other's way. You've seen that same thing before, mostly marriages where each partner just puts up with the other one.

As Jim and the boy put all the gear in the old truck, the old man said to the boy with a little chuckle, "Your gear looks like mine—small and old. But that's okay. That ain't what it's all about anyway."

The boy really didn't have much tackle, but he did have an Alcedo Micron Reel from France and a tiny fiberglass rod—four feet—and he used four-pound test. Of course, it had belonged to Jim but was a whim and had been discarded some time back, and for $8 or $9, the boy treasured it for years. His tackle box was homemade and given to him from Uncle Lester an aunt's second husband. The box was stuffed full of old River Runts, Dalton Specials, Bombers and 66 Specials, Creek Chubs, and a few homemade lures. All the tackle had been bought by the boy with money that he had earned from summer jobs, so losing a lure was utmost in his mind and his casting had to be accurate. Jim would take chances with his casting and would lose several lures every outing, but the boy seldom lost one because of the cost.

Soon they were rumbling down a gravel road, going

northwest in the dark. The sky was clear, and the North Star was very clear, up from the Dipper. The old man never got the old truck up to twenty miles per hour and seldom changed gears—mostly rode in second. What seemed like a lifetime finally came to an end when the old man declared, "We're here."

There was no breeze or sound but the river running beneath the old bridge the truck had stopped on. He ran to the edge and looked over. It was narrow and quicker than even Jim thought. He caught a little smell of firewood burning but thought no more of it.

Mr. Huff told both time was short. "This is really a 1½—2-day float. Even in the summer with short days, you won't have any time to dally, and don't hit that shoot—where that man lost his life—late 'cause you won't see it coming."

Whew, the boy thought, *that scares the shit out of me just thinking about it.*

Again the old man read his mind and said, "It wasn't a pretty sight, and I had to pull him from under that pile-up and he was buggered up pretty bad. It happens on the river," he said.

The old man said it like it had more than one meaning 'cause then he looked into the boy's eyes, and for a split second, the boy could feel his pain and his thoughts. He had lost someone close to him long ago—maybe a son or daughter. He never knew, but the loss was real to them both.

A pat on his shoulder meant it was time to take the river boat to water. There was a ring on the front and rear with a foot or so of cotton rope with a knot in the end so's you wouldn't drop your end. The boy was told to get on the front, and even though the boat was light, there was pressure on the boy's leg on the way down the steep slope alongside the bridge abutment. Everything went okay 'til halfway down and Jim's footing slipped and he lost hold of the rope. The boat came down on the boy's right leg and up the back of his thigh, sending boy, boat, pots and pans and fishing gear down the side of the bridge. The whole show took a turn and went under the bridge. That's when the memory of the wood smoke took on a whole new meaning 'cause he wound up looking at two old darkies eye-to-eye cooking on an open fire. Neither the darkies nor the boy moved for a while and finally an old darkie helped pick him up. He noticed they were cooking in an old hubcap and had fried up some fish and doggers (fried meat or grits in a ball). He had resprained his ankle he had been nursing for a month and began wiping blood running down the back of his leg.

Jim called out (after he had gathered himself), "You all right?"

The boy yelled out, "Hot damn, Jim, you run me down a bank. Hurt my leg and run smack dab into two darkies. Hell, no, I ain't all right!"

He crawled out madder 'n a hornet to meet the eyes of Mr. Huff who said, "Don't like darkies, huh?"

"Not much," the boy replied.

"They're okay. Old bucks are different," he said.

"If you say so," said the boy as he calmed down a bit.

He went to the river to clean the scrapes and cuts and stuck his ankle into the ice-cold water. His ankle was beginning to swell bad and hurt like hell, but he didn't say much. By this time, Jim had everything ready to put into the boat and was getting impatient to leave.

The boy started to put his stuff into the front when Jim said, "Go to the back. You're ready."

"Are you sure, Jim? That water is awful quick. I ain't

never been in water that quick and 'sides, that boat's new and I don't want anything bad to happen to it."

The old man called down to the boy to come up to him. The boy made his way up the bank somehow 'cause that ankle was really throbbing now. They met at the corner, and he could tell he was hurting pretty bad.

"Boy, you'll be okay. You got to push hard 'cause he will try to hit all the pops, but don't let him. You got to hit that bad shoot before dark 'cause I don't want to pull you out."

The boy asked, "How will I know what to do and which fork to take?"

"Remember, not always the biggest road's the best nor the biggest shoot winds up where you need to go. You'll know, and I can tell. See you tonight when I get back from Arkansas, after picking up three boat loads on a three-day trip—Yankees from St. Louis. Beer-drinking sons-of-bitches," he said.

By the time the boy reached the back of the boat and got his paddle, the truck and old man were rumbling out of sight. He somehow felt lonesome for him but couldn't figure how come. Light was up now and time to go said Jim. The boy waded out into the cold water and looked up into the sky—deep cobalt blue, no clouds, a perfect Canadian high. *One of them special days,* he thought, as he pushed south. With a little dig of the paddle, the long boat responded so quick he was into the shoot and down it so easy he couldn't believe it.

Jim turned around and said, "Told you you could handle it. Get on down one-half mile and pull over and we'll catch some red horses." (River minnows.)

The sun was warm and the air cool. *Just right,* thought the boy. He suddenly had a need to be close to his mom and grandmom. He missed them then, and many times to come would think of them in this setting.

Six or so mallards jumped as they went around a sharp bend but pitched back in as soon as the boat got through the pool. The boy thought to himself, *Everything is in order here except when man comes through it.* Kind of like he would like his life to be—a positive direction, not like his no-clear-cut way, a wandering effort, been nowhere but going nowhere faster. Most of the boys on the basketball team had some way or what they wanted to do in their minds enough to at least talk about, but the boy was so uncertain about the future he didn't even think about things much further than the end of a shotgun or rod tip.

Birds darted in front of the boat—kingfishers, crows, snipes. He thought about floating for ducks or squirrels someday and camping on a bar. He had a jungle hammock he used in the bottoms back home when he hunted squirrels. It would be perfect for a one-man float trip. Funny, he thought to himself about a float alone with no one to share all this with, but he felt more at ease while alone than with people. They just made things uncomfortable for him. They just didn't see nature like him. He was beginning to see well beyond his years about what it's like to take the life of some fish or duck and to know the feeling of taking a good fish or drake mallard and then looking at the dead object and wondering about the life it had lived or where it came from and the feelings of respect for that critter. There had been many times that year when he would let doves or squirrels pass and not take a shot but knowing inside he could have killed it anytime he wanted to. He was beginning to mature as a man, but more important, he was beginning to take responsibility for his actions.

Jim's voice startled the boy, who was deep inside himself.

"Pull over to that bar."

"You sure, Jim?"

"Yeah," he said, "I see some red horses up yonder in that slack water."

"Jim, don't you see that cottonmouth sunning?"

About the time Jim saw the snake, it went for the water and lay on the sandy bottom.

"Break his back!" Jim yelled.

So the boy picked up an extra paddle and aimed for the thickest part of the snake's body. He hit as hard as he could and felt the end of the paddle hit the thick body, sending it and snake deep into the sandy bottom. He knew this wouldn't kill the thing but keep it from moving so fast. He recalled how Joe Cummins taught him how to kill snakes on Swan Pond. "When they pile off in a boat, they always take a second or two to survey the situation. That's when you better get him," he said.

In a couple of seconds, he was watching the maddest snake he had ever seen. He was four feet and very thick and black. His mouth was as white as that ball of cotton on Mr. Huffsteadler's store and coming straight for the boy. He waited for that split second when it laid its head over the shallow boat's gunnel to see what its next move would be, but the snake didn't wait that second or two. It knew exactly its next move. So the boy laid the paddle to the neck about six inches back from the head and with that hard blow, the snake fell back into the river and started its death-rolling on the surface.

Jim turned around in the deck chair and said, "Hell of a job. Where did you learn that?"

"An old man showed me that move a couple of years ago at Swan Pond."

"If it's involving killing something, he's a good teacher," Jim replied and muttered a few cuss words about the old man. "Go to the next bar. Don't want to run into a sister or brother" (referring to the snake).

When they put out the "minner" jar, the boy laid down on the bar and rested in the sun. He took his jumper and made a pillow for his head. When they stopped moving, it was too warm, but when the boat moved on, it would get cool again. He thought about the odor of that cottonmouth. It was so dark he could hardly make out the blotchy bands. The belly was an unusual gray color with no markings. He remembered the small green-colored red horses he vomited when he broke his back from the first blow. *How old was he? Wonder if he had ever bothered anybody? After all, he wasn't bothering us,* he thought.

Every so often, he would look over at the glass jug to see the cracker crumbs boiling up with all the minnows trying to get out and finally said to Jim, "She full to the brim. Let's get them browns."

The boy pushed the boat away from the bar and into the current. Jim held the boat 'til the boy baited up by pulling a 3-ought hook through the minner's mouth and hooking it through the side and pulling up the slack, which made the minner turn in the water in a flashing manner. Pulled on top, it was deadly on browns 'cause of the tapping sound. It really pissed a big ol' brown off, and they could come a long way to smack it. Jim baited up and began hitting every possible hangout he saw, but remembered what the old man said, the boy began to move the boat at a faster clip. Jim said to slow down, but the boy just continued on. Jim had two fat browns when the boy cast to a spot Jim had missed. The minner hit the water and was immediately on top when the fish hit. It was a big rainbow. He tail-walked around the boat and back again before burrowing deep in a large pool for a down tree. As fast as he hit and struggled, he was gone, leaving the boy with a limp line and an expression of disbelief.

"What was that thing, Jim?"

"Big 'bow," he said. "Must have been ten pounds."

"Looked more like forty to me," said the boy with a big wide grin. "Did you see those colors and that tail-walk? I'm just glad to have a rod left. Mr. Huff said 'bows were in here but didn't say how big they were."

A shoot was coming up when he saw movement in the water below. He ran the boat in sand, jumped out, and ran up to the head of the shoot, lying on the ground so as not to spook the fish. He saw about a dozen big rainbow in the 5 to 10 pound range just hanging in the current and occasionally darting right or left to grab a minnow or sculpin. After a short time admiring the big 'bows, they moved on, picking up a few big browns and lots of small ones.

The boy's mind drifted back in the past—thinking none of the people who were close to him had ever seen these sights. He deducted they had been so busy at home they missed a lot of good things close to home. He vowed to himself not to get into a rut when he got older and limit himself on seeing other things rather than the backside of Kate and Beck—the family mules—or a radiator knob of a red belly Ford tractor. They passed several large springs and sampled the water, which was cold as ice. Every time a spring entered the river, it made it stronger and quicker.

There was a long stretch of smooth water and at the end was this golden glow. As the boat got closer, he could see the outline of the old beech trees with their gnarly limbs. As they entered the beech grove, the trees lined the river on both sides, with a massive old beech extending out over the water halfway across and a sister tree on the other side leaning over to form an arch. As they went under the trees, a breeze came through, sending millions of golden leaves through the air. There were millions covering the slopes and sand bars. They covered the water logs and every piece of land. Two old farmers were cooking "sargum," and he could see one man feeding the crusher and an old mule going around in circles. The aroma of the sargum and the smell of all the leaves made the most mellow smell he had ever smelled. All of the sights, sounds and smells began to well up inside the boy, and a great sense of peace suddenly came over him. His eyes began to well up with tears. He gently laid his paddle on the gunnel of the boat and just let the current pull the boat along. He had this overpowering feeling come over him that he had been here before or felt this overwhelming experience before.

Another breeze pushed thousands of leaves into the air, and the boy caught one and looked at it for a long time. It was perfectly formed and more golden than any of the others. He opened his small green tackle box and placed it in an empty tray. He wondered how he caught that perfect leaf and how much more perfect it was than all the rest. The leaf would stay in the box until he married. He thought of his girlfriend and felt a love for her that was more even than for his kin. A longing came over him, and he knew that the leaf represented her. He was amazed while sitting in this special place that she could choose him over others who were more outgoing and popular. He would tell her of these happenings in the winter of their lives on down the river.

The leaves began to represent everything beautiful in the world and in his life. He peered down into the dark deep pool, and the bottom was strewn with millions of leaves. Some were darker yellow and some lighter, depending on how long they lay there. As the current caught leaves from all stratas, he saw leaves torn in halves, quarters, stems, tips. Some had been in the water for days with a mossy appearance. The river had taken its toll—maybe like the river of life.

Jim was getting antsy due to the browns coming up and hitting the red horse but not getting hooked, but the boy paid little attention because he was lost in the moment. Way too soon for the boy, the boat was coming to the tail of the pool. Just before they went over the shoal and down the shoot, the boy looked back for a last time, and another feeling came to him from the past. A feeling of reluctance to leave and urgency to move forward came over him and then it was gone as the boat went down the shoot that broke to the left. He was accompanied by thousands of floating leaves dancing on the surface as far as he could see. He said to himself, *This must be the most beautiful sight I have ever seen.* He would grow up and travel and see many churches and cathedrals, but none would surpass what he had just seen nor would the feeling ever match what he had felt.

As the boat entered the next pool, it, too, was covered with golden leaves. They were everywhere, but more could be seen in the currents below, broken and discolored. As the boils and currents took heavy tolls on the leaves, the boy noted all the subtle changes going on below and watched as the currents had their way with the leaves on the surface. They were swept in and around the boils and turbulence, pushed here and there, and were at the mercy of the currents. He could not get over how many there were. After moving from pool to pool, he wondered how some of the leaves fought to stay afloat, and they seemed to be playing tag, going this way and that way, but as they floated along, there were fewer now, and after about a mile or so, they numbered only in the hundreds. The boy knew eventually there would be none, and he wished he could go back and see this all over again, but it was impossible to go upstream, and time was becoming a big factor now as night comes quickly this time of year, especially on the river deep in hill country.

Jim grew more and more impatient and complained out loud about the leaves interfering with his fishing. *How could anybody cuss what I just saw? How could he not feel anything for the beauty we have seen?* And then he remembered what a very wise man told him a long time ago. "There are givers and takers. Be sure you are a giver," his granddaddy told him. Jim wanted to take fish; that was his reason for being there. The boy couldn't give anything, but he took what he was destined to take—a feeling about life and what it means while on the river. *How different we all are and how we see things and how we feel about things around us in our makeup. We can change little,* thought the boy. *It's just his nature. It doesn't mean he's bad. He just responds to different things than I do,* he thought. He laid his rod down and didn't fish anymore that trip. Jim didn't even notice the boy not fishing; he was totally focused on what he was doing. The boy marveled at how good he was—years and years of practice and experience. He was a master fisherman. Maybe he would reflect on what he saw in his own mind or talk about the beauty another time. Surely he saw the beauty of all this. It couldn't just be the browns. The boy never found the answers to his questions about Jim. He would always be a mystery to him. They would eventually drift apart in the future, but the boy always respected him for his abilities. Jim seemed to become more and more involved with other people who shared interest in larger and different types of fish. The boy would pursue the brown until he became an old man—who still preferred moving water to lakes and still was very content in the back of the boat.

A mile or so down river, the boy observed the last of the floating leaves moving at a fast clip in the main current. Each fighting to stay afloat and in front, first one then another would gain the lead, some dropping out to get caught on a limb or object beneath the surface. He watched as three in a row began to sink, then two and finally one left. It had been in the water a long time, half afloat and half sunk. It fought as long as it could but finally the current won and the leaf was lost forever—but not to the boy. It would return soon enough on down his river.

The boy wondered about the last bunch of leaves. *How come they got to go so far? What set them apart from all the rest? Why was the last one any different from the first? Or did it matter? What if they had all sunk in the first pool and just gave up?* But he remembered how they seemed to struggle—not wanting to sink. It was like they were trying to keep a beautiful thing alive as long as they could because the end was so final. He wondered if anybody else had seen this same thing over the years. He just could not shake the leaves from his mind. What had been reluctance to sit in the back now came so easy the boy had nothing but time to remember the leaves. It was like he had been doing this all his life. He was gifted in insight in the currents and how to read them and how to make the boat respond to his command.

It was getting late in the day when he heard the rapids ahead, and he knew it was the ones that had killed the man a week before. Something inside told him to take the small shoot to the left even though the strong current wanted the boat to go right. He thought to himself, *There are many followers in life.* He had seen this in fellow classmates, but he knew this was not a proper choice.

Jim turned around and asked, "What are you doing?"

The boy jumped into the cold water, pushed the front end to make it over a shallow shoal, and sent them down a narrow chute barely wide enough for the boat to go. Had the river been low, they would have had to pull over a dry shoal.

At the end of the shoot, Jim said, "Let's walk back and take a look at that mean piece of shit."

As they walked back up the gravel shoal, Jim said to the boy, "How did you know which one to take, being you've never seen it before?"

The boy's remark was never acknowledged by Jim, but the boy had seen wide and narrow spots before, but there was something else unexplainable going on inside of him. He was beginning to draw from the leaves and didn't even know about the insight.

They watched the river boil and roll over boulders, trees and debris from the spring rains. *Unbelievable power,* thought the boy. *Something you just can't stop,* he thought. But then he hadn't seen what man had done to the White River a few miles west. The dams man had placed in wild rivers had tamed them to the place they were destroyed forever and could not return to their natural state. Progress marches on; be quick to seize the moment 'cause it may never return or if it does, you may not be there to see it.

Darkness was closing fast as the boat hit the sand at Riverton late that afternoon, and the boy was dead tired. The boy pulled the boat up, and when Jim got out with all the gear, he flipped the boat over to let it drain. He immediately looked at the bottom. There were some scuffs and knocks and scratches but not too bad considering the elements it had passed over. Boats always amazed him on how much weight they could float and punishment they could take, but this one had become dear because of the ride through which they both had made it together. He had memorized the whole interior—every nail and board and how they fit—and how it swept across the surface of water so easily. He wished he could meet the man who had made the craft but knew Mr. Huff had designed it, so that was good enough for him.

Jim took all the gear up to camp and began to start supper.

"Get them browns out and start cleaning them," Jim ordered.

The boy got an old coal-oil lantern from the car and lit it. A yellow light soon glowed—just light enough to see but not too much. He put his jumper on and grabbed the fish and paddle and began to fillet the browns using the paddle blade as a table. He didn't hear the old man approach but knew he was near. He looked up to see him walk within a few feet of Jim, but Jim didn't see him.

He strolled up and with a soft voice said, "Mind if I sit and talk a spell?"

The boy threw him an old boat cushion, and a conversation like he had never heard before started. It wasn't like the boy hadn't talked to the old folks before; he had many times. Mostly the old would talk and kids listened, but this was going to be different. It was like both of them were going down a chute and had just so much time to get it said.

The old man started by saying, "Did you enjoy the day?"

The boy said, "It was the greatest day of my life." *Funny,* he thought, *I was never able to say something like that before.* "Mr. Huff, I'm sorry but I put some knocks and scrapes on your boat."

The old man looked at the bottom of his boat.

"It's okay. You're going to get that while you're on the river—builds character."

Somehow he didn't think he was talking about the same boat or river. With a twinkle in his eye and in the soft glow of the lantern, he could tell the old man was going to set many of the boy's questions to rest. The questions began to roll out of the boy until he asked about the leaves. The old man's face changed like he had a great weight lifted off him.

The boy said, "I just can't get them out of my thoughts."

"Tell me about them," he said with a grin. And the boy related all he had seen and about the two distinct feelings he had felt.

The old man said, "I saw those same leaves when I was about your age, and I couldn't forget them either. After all these years, I can still remember them and the effect they had on me. You are the only one who had ever said anything about them all these years."

"What does it mean?" asked the boy.

"I'll tell you about the first feeling. Was it a sense of peace?"

"Yes," the boy said, "like I have never known—like in church but not the same. I don't know; it frustrates me."

The old man leaned back and said, "When you entered the grove, it represents when you were in your mother—warm, glowing, full of life, a feeling of peace. You will experience this again on down river."

Puzzled, he went to the second feeling, which was the longing for the past but knowing he had to move on.

"Study about what you saw and that feeling, and you will know for yourself without me telling you."

The boy closed his eyes. He was completely uninhibited by the old man by this time and thought of the leaves in the pool and how they moved along farther from the mother trees and how they were swept way down the chute never to go back. And in an instant, the both knew what that feeling was he had had so long ago. It was time for the little boy's first day at school. He and Mama Mills had talked about it for weeks.

All the preparation for that first day—the new homemade shirt with undershorts to match; the whiz-bang mash feed sacks she and he had so carefully picked out; all the hours of sewing she had done—and then it was time to go to catch the bus. They both silently walked to the road, and the big yellow bus slowed and finally stopped. He climbed on board, and as it left, he ran to the back and looked out the dusty old windows at her waving at him. He waved back until she was out of sight and the bus moved on. He wanted to stay home on the farm but knew he couldn't.

The river rolls on. That afternoon she was waiting at the road, and she asked all about his day at school and he told her, but somehow he knew things had changed and he had missed a day at home. He related all this to the old man, and he became very solemn. He knew all too well the feelings of the boy. It was a very tense time for them both. Finally the old man said—after a long pause—how he must depend on the leaves like a road map and how great things were in store for the boy but, "you must rely on them because they had special meaning just for you."

The boy had so many questions that Mr. Huff finally said, "Just shut your eyes and think of the river, the leaves, and all you'll need to figure the answers will come."

He patted the boy on the shoulder and got up to leave. Just like when the boy looked back at the pool and the leaves for the last time, the old man stood and gazed in the direction of the boy, the boat and the river beyond and smiled.

He said, "I'll talk to you again some day on down the river." As quickly as he came, he was gone.

Jim hollered out to the boy and asked, "Who you talking to and where's the fish? I could have dressed all the fish in the river by now."

The boy never said a word and handed Jim the fillets.

After the trip to the point began to fade with time, the boy would return to the point but never saw Mr. Huff. He was always out on a boat haul or something. He missed seeing him but couldn't help it. As he entered the last of the spring of his school life, he tried to play ball and go to school and learn to fit into this new society. With not much success on any of the three, he was beginning to drift again. But before going to college, he began to think of marriage, and he felt that all that had taken place and had been said should be placed in the past and forgotten. So he and his new bride left for school. He was entering the fastest and deepest water of his life, and as he went on, he would think at times about his ball playing, coach and high school failures. He was thinking about his lack of playing time and began to think of the leaves on the logs and how they observed the rest floating in the river. He thought, *That must be referring to me,* but then a thought came to him that he would enter a new game in which he would start every game, play every play, and win more than he would lose. He soon would forget that and drifted again into himself. He would soon become a parent, and more responsibility would come.

As he began to compete with more and much smarter people, he began to feel more and more inadequate. As he was studying late one night on histology, he laid his head down on the table and thought to himself. This teacher talked him into taking the senior course before he had two others and told him he could do it fine, but the students were way above average even for seniors. He began to again think of the leaves; it was the only place he could go in his mind and be comfortable. He said to himself, *How can I compete with all these smart people and me not having the courses I need to have?* A voice began to talk to him. He sat up and looked around. Everybody was asleep but him. He thought, *I know it's late and I'm tired but I know I heard Daddy Mills speak.* The voice began to speak again. *You must outwork them. I wasn't as smart as some of the others around me, so I just outworked them.* This was early summer in the young man's life, and already he could see that very intelligent people who had high IQs also had flaws; they tended to be lazy. So he would spend more time on studies and stay late in labs, and the results began to pay off for him. His grades improved, and soon he was given the honor of being asked by his peers to be in honor societies.

As the last year of college flew by, he was accepted into a doctoral program in a large city, and again he was placed in with smarter and stronger students. Again he began to rely on the leaves. Each time they spoke, the voices came from his past—Ruth, Trevor, Cousin Luther, Uncle Lenny, Mary Lee, Mama Mills, Daddy Mills, Eurlene Perry, Vernon Perry, on and on—all from the past but clear as the point's running water. The answers given wouldn't be direct answers but were given in areas or abstracts that made him think about the rules and old ways taught by the people who had meant so much to him as a boy. And the answers flowed down just like the leaves from the beech trees on the point. They got him through with honors, and even though they were all smarter, he stuck to the old rules and outworked them all. He began to feel he had an unfair advantage and it wasn't fair for him to have the answers, but it was then he would make mistakes in the fall of his life and he remembered Mr. Huff's voice saying, "They're your road map; rely on them."

In the fall of his life, he noticed on the appointment book the name of his old coach. The old coach was a bully of a man but was still held in great respect around the state. But the doctor remembered him for what he didn't do or say more than for his accomplishments. He dreaded seeing him again, and he knew he would say something cutting. He wasn't worried about what the coach would say but rather what might be said on his part or how he would feel after the appointment because he had had a very negative effect on him, and he had the mental scars to prove it. So he went to the leaves, and they told him the answer. Cousin Luther had a rapier tongue and could put anybody in their place if need be.

So when the coach came, sure enough he looked right at the doctor and said, "I hope you're better at this than as a ball player."

Without any hesitation, he stated, "I was a better ball player than you were a friend, Coach."

"Well, get on with it," said the coach, and the procedure was completed. There were never any words spoken between them again, and even though he was a man, the boy inside lost the fear of ever being in anyone's shadow forever.

So as he entered the winter of his life, times were tough but he relied solely on the leaves for answers and direction. They were always there for him, but he was beginning to use all of them now. As he moved on down the river, many currents and turbulences were beginning to tear at his body and mind, and questions were aimed at his old ways and teachings. He was sitting watching his cattle one evening and drifted back to the leaves. He saw three leaves tailing one another, and they began to touch one another, and Ruth spoke and said, *The leaves represent Family, Work, and Responsibility.* In the middle was the sun sparkling, which represented Religion, and he knew his ways were correct. Just because others didn't recognize his teachings didn't mean they were wrong.

Not far after that, he was again puzzled about life. So he questioned the leaves—this being the first time he would ask for a direct answer. There were two leaves floating along the stream, and they were drawn to one another. *What does it mean?* A voice from the past—Mama Mills—said, *You are responsible for everything you touch or come in contact with to do your best. Responsibility is the answer to life.* And some time went by, and finally he saw the one leaf—the same one he saw so long ago trying to stay afloat—and he asked again, *What does it mean?* Mr. Huff slowly spoke and said, *I told you I would speak to you on down the river. You will float the point again alone. This time you will drift upon a sand bar, and the old boat will come to rest. You will get out and lay on the bar. Your son will become the father, and you will become childlike. Your son will get into the back of the boat, and your grandchildren will get in the front. You will look to your left and see bare beech trees, but look closely. Millions of buds are ready for next spring's leaves. As you look back at the boat with your boy guiding his children, they will look back*

and wave to you, and they will go over the shoal and down the chute, and a great peace will come over you.

How will I know what to do now that all the leaves are gone?

You will know all the secrets of the leaves. You won't need a road map where you are going.

Dear Son,
It's been an honor to share my stretch of the river with you. When I'm gone and you climb in the back of the boat where I've sat for years, a small part of me will always be there with you.
Remember the leaves. Pop.

Road Maps for Old Mules, Old Wagons, and Little Boys

It was a cold, windy November day. It had been drizzling rain off and on and, every now and then, spitting snow. The boy was given the job by his granddad of oiling the old harness and lines to be used the next day to take off the last load of cotton to town. The old granddad had just finished greasing all the wagon wheels with axle grease and was wiping his hands off on some hay when he told the boy to feed the mules after he got through with that chore. The boy noticed the grease went into all the cuts and lines in the old man's hand—looking like a kind of road map he had seen one time at his Uncle Clyde's house.

After the boy put up the old harness in the side room, he climbed up into the barn and went into the corncrib. Mice scurried right and left as he entered this old dry room. The smell of earcorn is a dry mellow smell. Coupled with mouse urine and dust, it makes for an unusual smell at best. Then a combination of warm cattle, mules, hay and manure makes for a smell only country folks can appreciate and long for those days of old. He placed four ears of corn in the old woven basket along with several nubbins and went to the stalls of old Beck and Kate. Speaking softly to each mule as only a boy can, he gave them their corn with a couple of extra nubbins for the long haul tomorrow. He looked deep in the sad old brown eyes and wondered what they thought about and if they liked him as much as he cared for them. As he climbed down from the hall, the old man called to him to look at the sunset with him, and they both peered at the sight. The old man reminded him there would never be one exactly like this one.

"They are all different, like a curtain ending the final act of a play. Always look back and think about what you've done, and do better tomorrow," he said with a light pat on the boy's shoulder.

It was a sunset you just could not forget. The clouds were all shades of purple and yellows and backed up by gray—almost black—clouds rolling in from the northwest.

"It'll be another cold one coming in, but no rain," he said with a slight grin on his old wrinkled face.

He had seen many sunsets, and the boy guessed he knew what he was talking about. He never seemed to be wrong, and he tried to mimic all his moves and gestures—even the way he walked. Granddad was his idol. Most people in the community had given up farming with mules and the old ways, but he hung on to the past even to the end.

After all the chores were finished and they were going to the woodshed for wood for the fireplace and wood stove, the boy posed a question.

"How come we don't get a tractor like Clyde and Vernon?"

The old man, glancing away for a moment, said, "Well, I guess somebody ought to take care of Beck and Kate. They done such a good job, seem sad to do away with them now. Don't you think?"

"Yes, sir," said the boy. "Sure would miss them. I bet they're worth a hundred, 'specially old Kate. 'Member she rolled over last summer, and you said a mule who could roll over was worth a hundred."

The old man looked down at his grandson and smiled, and they gathered up the firewood for the evening.

Shortly after supper, the old man said, "Cook us some popcorn, boy."

That was all he needed. The boy sliced off two or three slices from a big slab of bacon hanging on the back porch and took a big gob of butter that always sat in the center of the old table along with the homegrown popcorn, placed it all in a hand-held popper and put it in the fireplace flames.

"Got to be popped 'fore Lum and Abner comes on," the old man said.

He turned to the battery-powered radio and began to fiddle with the dial. When he had it right, he left the room to go to the back porch to empty out 'cause they didn't have indoor plumbing. As the boy sat and waited for the first kernel to pop, he could hear the bacon sizzling and start to cook. When the last popcorn popped, he placed the corn in a big bowl just in time for the two old men from Pine Ridge to come on.

"Nothing better 'cept Mama's cooking," said the old feller.

The boy wasn't old enough to understand the humor of the radio show but played like he did. When Daddy Mills laughed, he would laugh. They would sit there for hours listening to Amos and Andy, Fibber McGee, the Grand Old Opry 'til all the corn was gone.

Finally, Mama Mills came in and said, "Albert, you and Jerry Boy better scoot off to bed. Got a big day tomorrow."

She had taken some old cast irons and heated them near the fireplace to put in the feather bed so's it would be warm 'cause there wasn't a stove where the boy slept.

The old granddad hitched up the mules to the wagon full of cotton before daylight and drove the rig up to the house. He and the boy ate a big breakfast. They wouldn't eat again 'til they got home a little before dark. He ran to the old wagon and pulled up a big wad of cotton over a thin plank for a seat.

Mama Mills came out of the side porch with him, and he got upon the big wagon and told the boy, "Cluck 'em up, boy."

Mama Mills said with a grin, "You boys need a road map how to get there and back."

"No, ma'am, old Kate knows the way."

Wonder why she said that, he thought. With a soft cluck, the boy drove the team down the lane to the edge of the road. The steel rims mashed small gravel and broke some of the little rocks. What a feeling to drive the team with the cotton he helped pick! With a quick glance at his granddad's hands, he saw the stained lines and nicks and scrapes of his old wrinkled hands that had picked nearly all the cotton except for the small sacks the boy contributed to the load. He saw a small trickle of blood from a cut run down to the old man's nail, so the boy scuffed a scab and soon had some blood showing, which made him feel like a part of the show. And a show it was, even back then. That cotton patch was the most northern one grown, his granddad told him, but that was soon to change.

When they pulled up to the main road, he told the boy, "I'll drive now. You watch for cars and trucks coming up behind us so I can talk to ol' Beck."

She was so scared of trucks that they had to put her on the outside, but she was just as bad on bridges, so it was a tradeoff. As they rumbled down the road, they went by kinfolk's places and friend's farms. They had just passed the Springhill Y when Uncle Lenny pulled out on the road in an old, old black car ahead of the old team and wagon. But almost as soon as he got on the road, he started sidling off on the shoulder; he had seen Luther Lampkin in the middle of a field with some milk cans, so Uncle Lenny began to walk and talk at the same time 'til they met and began to strike up a conversation. He was known in those parts for that characteristic.

As the team went past the two old gentlemen, the old granddad turned to the boy and said, "I bet he never makes it to town today."

The boy nodded 'cause he had seen this scene before. One time they went to town to the feed mill and came back home and Uncle Lenny was still talking in the middle of another field. They both laughed, and the boy clucked to the old team and they slowly moved on. All the way to town, they talked about gettin' home and milkin' and feedin' and then cookin' some more corn and then listenin' to the Opry. Time passes fast when you're having fun, and 'fore long, it was time to turn off to the gin.

When they pulled up to the gin, there were ten or so darkies unloading wagons like theirs and a lot of trucks. It was like you could see into the future. *Times are a-changing,* thought the boy, but his granddad sat on the wagon board frozen in time, never to go forward but always backward as progress pressed on. He went into the weight room, and they cut him a check for a whole crop: $180.00.

The boy ran up to his granddad and asked, "How much we get?"

"Nuff," said the old man.

"Boy, that's a lot," said the boy.

But the old fellow just looked away and said, "Time to go wash the cuff, Jerry Boy."

"What's that?"

"Well, we got to go by Baco's feed store first. 'Member all them feed sacks and layin' mash?" he said. "Well, it was on the cuff and we got to wash it clean."

As the old wagon pulled up to the old feed store, the boy jumped off to see if any of the prints on the layin' mash sacks had changed from last summer when he and Mama Mills picked out the ones to make him some new shirts and underwear for the new school year. As his eyes skimmed the dusty sacks, he spied a new batch of whiz-bang colors. *Got to tell Mama Mills new ones come in.* Maybe he could have a new shirt, he thought. He wandered over to the room where the incubator was where all the baby chickens were hatched. They would come in the spring and get one hundred baby chicks. He remembered the little balls of fluff, and a good feeling came over him. The smells of all the feeds, sacks, dust, corn were similar to the barn at home but not the same, he thought. Out of the corner of his eye, he saw Daddy Mills shake Mr. Baco's hand, and he ran to the wagon to help cluck up the team. They headed toward Brummels Grocery. As they neared Daddy Ned's blacksmith barn, they pulled in behind the shed.

"Mind if the team stay here while I go to Brummels?" Daddy Mills asked Daddy Ned.

A nod meant okay, so they strolled down to the store. The boy knew he would get a creme cone and went right to the fountain area while Daddy Mills went to wash the cuff. After polishing off the cone, they strolled west to U Totems and paid off a little jag of the bill and went back to the wagon.

As they climbed aboard, the boy turned to the old man and asked, "Cuff clean now, Daddy Mills?"

"Clean as it's gonna' get." He grinned.

They turned the rig back toward home. They were

both getting weary and spoke little 'til they saw Uncle Lenny talking to another farmer. They both smiled at each other, and Daddy Mills said, "Hope he wasn't supposed to go to Brummels for bread."

They both laughed. It was gettin' late as they pulled into the lane. Mama Mills was looking out the window where the two stars still hung showing where her sons were in the service. Daddy Mills climbed down to meet her. They spoke in quiet tones the boy couldn't hear. He handed her $22. That was all that was left. She pulled him over and gave him a peck on the cheek and a soft pat on the back. They both seemed so sad, thought the boy.

The old man said, "Take the rig to the barn and I'll be there directly."

The boy clucked to the mules, and the whole rig moved west toward the setting sun. He took a little longer watching it set today. He didn't see Daddy Mills but sensed he was near.

"How many ears do I feed old Beck and Kate?" he asked, knowing the answer.

"Same as yesterday," he said soft and low. "It's good to be back home."

After they got through milking, they headed towards the house. A coal-oil lamp could barely be seen but was enough to get home by.

Daddy Mills said, "Some of that corn would be good whiles we listen to the Opry."

"Coming right up." The boy ran on ahead to the back porch to get the bacon. *Same as yesterday,* he thought.

* * *

It was late spring (May, I think). The boy was standing by the old pump Singer sewing machine. Mama Mills had been sewing for quite a while now, and the boy began to wonder.

"What in the world are those things for?"

The old woman stopped and with a sad look on her face said, "You 'member when you saw that troop train stop down at the trestle the other day when you and Daddy Mills were going to the sleepy field on the west side of the track?"

"Yes, ma'am," said the boy. "I can still see their faces pressed against the glass. They looked so sad."

"They *were* sad," she said. "They were agoin' where Clarence is to fight the Germans."

The boy thought awhile.

"Think they will see him over there?"

She had spent some time teaching him where they were fighting with the globe in the parlor.

"Maybe. You never know," she said. "Maybe it will be over time they get there, but they will be hungry. That's where we the farmers come in."

Puzzled, the boy thought for a while.

Mama Mills would read the war news to him every day, and they would listen to Gabriel Heater every night on the radio about what was happening on the front lines.

" 'Member the picture in the paper of the tired and hungry soldier boys?"

"Yes, ma'am," he said.

"Well, we all have to sacrifice at home for the war efforts—like the victory gardens, your little saving stamp book—and to answer your question, we have to send the lambs so the soldier boys will have something to eat. These bonnets will go over their heads tomorrow when you and Daddy Mills take them to Mr. Roy's to sell for the war effort."

"Not Wooly!" said the boy.

He was an orphaned lamb they had given the boy. He fed Wooly bottled milk from old Doo Dinner, the cow he milked. The lamb was always smaller and weaker 'til the last month, and he grew almost as big as the other lambs.

"Yes," Mama Mills said. "He must go, too."

The boy wanted his bonnet to be special, so she sewed a little red yarn tassel on it for the boy, who wandered off alone where Daddy Mills was rocking in front of the fireplace.

"Daddy Mills, will they hurt Wooly?" he asked in a low voice.

"No, they always take special care of all the lambs who go to our service boys."

The boy looked deep into the flames for a long time, thinking about all the boys on the train and finally convinced himself it would be okay. He had only seen hogs killed in the fall but didn't think it would be the same.

The next morning they hitched up the team and then placed the bonnets on the lambs. The boy put the last bonnet on Wooly and spoke softly in his ear—"Be a good boy over there"—and quickly tied the red string around the back of the lamb's head. He wouldn't ever see him again, refusing to look in the lamb's direction on the way to town and when they unloaded them at Mr. Roy's. The boy walked down the road a ways. The old wagon made the old familiar route: Baco, Brummels, U Totems, and back to the farm. The road map was completed again.

As the boy stands in the doorway of the barn, he hears the old sounds of the wind moaning through the cracks and lifting up the smells inside the barn. The sun is setting deep in the southwest with brilliant colors changing all around him, and the old gentle hand pats him on the shoulder and says, "Just like yesterday."

* * *

It's summer, and the sun is just coming up. Mama Mills has the dinner bucket full with fried chicken, boiled eggs, and huge ripe tomatoes. This trip is to go to the saw mill Daddy Mills and Mr. Lonnie own at Springhill.

The old wagon creaks down the lane, and Mama Mills asks, "You all think you can find your way home?"

"Yes, ma'am," said the boy with a grin. "Kate can."

The smell of summer back then. Corn tassels. Weeds. High-moisture air. A smothering feeling when the sun's up.

It's only two or three miles to the mill, but the mules travel slowly past Cousin Luther's. The boy waves to Trevor and Miss Lissie sweeping the chicken yard. *Hope Mama Mills doesn't see them doing that,* thought the boy. *She'll have me doing that again.* Oh, how he hated that job 'cause tomorrow it would be back the same, he thought. They went past the old darkie Jence's place and on and on 'til they turned off the road to the old mill. When I say old, I mean old. It consisted of an old huge Case Trashing Engine. It burned wood to heat the water to make steam to turn the big wheel on the right side of the engine. To the boy, it looked like at least one-hundred belts went everywhere to turn the gears and make the whole show go.

They stopped the team under a huge scaly bark tree and gave them a drink from the mill pond. He always brought a cane pole to fishing the pond but never caught anything. I guess the old men hated to tell him there weren't any fish in it. He set out the line and went to the back of the engine where Mr. Lonnie was putting firewood in the fire box in the rear of the old Case engine. Hot was not the word for it. The humidity must have been 90 percent, and the whole area lay down in a holler, so the heat just lay there. He walked around to the carriage that carried the logs on their way to the big circular blade where Daddy Mills was sharpening the cutting points for the day's sawing, which would commence as soon as a full head of steam built up in the engine. With a couple of toots on the engine's whistle signaling time to start sawing, Daddy Mills pulled a log down onto the carriage and dogged it down. Then he would step back like the artist he was and in his mind determine how to cut out the boards he wanted. It was unexplainable how good he was at this, and most people said Albert's cuts didn't have "thick and thins" like other mills around them parts.

As the day wore on, the boy could only watch and play in the sawdust, but he also milled around the area watching the two old men working in the most hostile environment you could possibly imagine. Their shirts were blue cotton, and not a dry thread could you see. Sweat ran down their arms, and neither had an ounce of fat on their bodies. Just hard work—from sunup to sunset. The boy watched Mr. Hill cut firewood for the engine. With a flip of his hand, he engaged a belt that made a sling saw whine like it was a high-pitched yell. And when it went into the wood, it would go through like a knife through butter. The sound of the engine and both saws and all the belts moving was a sight you just couldn't forget. Dinnertime would come with a couple of toots of the whistle, and they would all gather under the big scaly bark with Beck and Kate and eat dinner. The mill was quiet except for the engine occasionally letting off steam and some puff of smoke out the stack.

Mr. Lonnie would walk back and twist a few valves, and life would slowly come back to the little show down in that old glen. And then it would start all over agin. As the day wore on, the wood pile would grow over a man's head, and the stacks of lumber Daddy Mills sawed grew to huge stacks, placed by Joe Featherstone, the offbearer. Finally around 6:00, Mr. Lonnie had one long blast on the whistle and started shutting down valves, and the old iron horse came to rest, sighing when steam and smoke slowed to a stop. It was as if it never really happened 'til you saw the big stacks of wood. It was—and still is—in the boy's mind quite a sight. As Daddy Mills got off the carriage, he motioned to the boy to bring the team over to load the wagon with firewood to be split for winter. As if working eleven hours wasn't enough, he had to load the wagon and then unload and feed and milk. The boy helped as much as he could, but the slabs were just too big, so he was relegated to loading kindlin'.

As they pulled away from the mill, the two paused to look back at the scene. It would be the last time 'cause it burned down some time in the night. Mr. Lonnie and Daddy Mills had just paid off a month before due to the first mill's same fate. It saddens me to think about it to this day—how people try and try and things just continue to go to shit. The old wagon creaks and groans on its way up the long hill heading home. The mules almost lie down and struggle getting up that long hill almost to a stop when Beck sees Kate can't pull anymore. She seemed to kick into a different gear and eased on up the hill. Jerry Peery and his dad pass with a nod and quick wave. They are always going by with that look of "a day late and a dollar short." They were going in their house for supper when the old rig rumbled by. It would be about an hour before dark, and they needed to get off the road 'cause they didn't have any lights. They hit the lane just as the sun was going down, and they unhitched the mules and watched the sunset.

"Guess they will need about two ears and some nubbins."

Just like yesterday, they both thought. *Just like yesterday.*

* * *

It's fall, and the final trip is carrying a load of corn to the mill in town to be ground and some molasses put in the mix. The big sideboards are put on to be able to carry more corn. They loaded the corn on Friday, and early Saturday they started to town. This would be the last wagon ride for the boy 'cause Daddy Mills was slowing down in his farming efforts.

Mama Mills came out to say, "Hope you all can find your way home."

This time the boy said, "We'll just read the lines (that look like a map) on Daddy Mills's hand to get back home."

We all laughed, and they pulled out to town. They went along watching folk picking corn and mending fences. It was a beautiful fall day with the sun punching holes in the clouds, the rays coming down to the ground and touching the dew on the withering grass and leaves. There had already been a couple of hard frosts, and the foliage had begun to turn like it had been done by an artist's brush. Brilliant colors were everywhere. It was a great time to be a young boy. They hardly spoke; they sensed what the others was thinking. They were that close. The old man pointed out sights that he thought were unusual or important with a nod in that direction and a nod for the boy indicating he understood. It's hard to believe they could be in tune that well, but it's true.

They finally got to the mill after two hours, and a couple of darkies went to work unloading the corn. The boy and Daddy Mills walked across the road to the Tuxcedo Bottling Company and watched the bottling process and bought six orange cold drinks to put over homemade ice cream Mama Mills made on occasion. Then they sauntered up the road to Mr. Roy Berry's stock yard to hear him spin a few yarns. Sometimes it's important not to have a job staring you in the face and just nonchalantly see and do a few things without thinking or doing work. The corn was now ground and put in sacks and placed back in the wagon, and they eased back up town to go to Brummels to get some lye for Mama Mills to make soap the next month come hog-killing time. They headed old Beck and Kate toward home in time to start milking and feeding. At that magical time of sunset, they met on the south side of the old barn with the familiar sound and smells emanating view the sunset and the same old questions.

"How many ears, Daddy Mills?"

"Two apiece," he said with a smile.

Same as yesterday, thought the boy.

* * *

All the wagon rides put together couldn't override the most important ride to church every Sunday. Mama Mills and Daddy Mills took the boy every Sunday that he lived with them, and the road map that was given to him always showed him the way home.

They're all gone now—Daddy Mills, Mama Mills, all the kinfolk up and down the road except Clarence, Bob, and Jerry Peery, and where once stood a young boy, an old man stands. His hands remind him of Daddy Mills's hands—wrinkled and plenty of road maps. He spends more and more time in the past now and revisits the old barn and the sunsets. The sights, sounds, and smells are still the same, as the old man looks back through the eyes of the boy still inside him. He thinks to himself, *Nothing has changed. Same as yesterday,* he thinks, as Daddy Mills puts his hand on his shoulder and says, "Same as yesterday, Jerry Boy."

Old Times Are Not Forgotten Look Away Dixieland

A while back, my dad and I were talking about old times, and he came out with the most unusual thought. He said, "The most enjoyable time of my life was when we were housing our tobacco crop to send the boys to college." I shuddered and said, "You've got to be kidding?" We all began to kid him about what he had said, and as usual, we soon heard the door close behind him as he shuffled off. He's eighty-six years old now, and we all just knew in the early stages of old-timer's disease 'cause working in tobacco has got to be the hardest, dirtiest, and hottest job known to mankind.

Some time has gone by now, and I think back to those times, and one occasion in particular. We had just hung the last stick of burly in the barn, and all the boys and I came rolling out of that hot box and lit down on the ground to see the smiling face of Daddy Bob, almost black with dirt and with small rivulets cutting through the grit and grime where the sweat had run down his face. All the boys went to the house along with Mammy to get a cold drink, and he and I eased off to put the last finishing touches to firing to finish the last dark fired job. I saw him glance back at the barn, just like he and his dad had many years ago, and he said, "Looks good, doesn't it? Remember how small all those plants were we put in a while back?" I mumbled some off-color answer and began to put the wood down for the firing. After an hour or so of putting sawdust down over the wood planks and limbs, we lit the fire and shut the doors to the old barn. As the smoke began to permeate the inside of the old timber, you could just begin to smell the unmistakable smell of sawdust, wood, and tobacco combining. We both watched as the smoke came out of the pecker wood holes and cracks of the wall, finally meandering on up out of the holes in the roof. He said, "Sad to see the end."

We began walking back to the house, but this time we both stopped and took a second or two to look back at the smoking old barn. Almost like what you think when an artist steps back to look at the last brush mark. We both felt the pride of doing our best. It may not have been the best tobacco at the sale that year, but it was the best we could do. He said to me, "When your boys go across the stage to get those diplomas, a little bit of us will be with them." We laughed and shuffled off towards home.

Now as I think back, it wasn't the tobacco season he was sorry to see end. It was our time together as family, working together for a common cause. Time has taken its toll on him and the family. I read somewhere one time where Henry David Thoreau put time in an eloquent framework. "Time," he said, "is but the stream I go a fishin' in. I drink at it; but while I drink, I see the sandy bottom and detect how shallow it is. Its thin current slides away, but eternity remains."

Old times are not forgotten. Look away Dixieland.

Thanks for all your time, Daddy Bob.

Petals and Dew from the Past

Not so long ago, a patient was chatting with Faye and myself about angels and happened to ask me if I had ever seen one. I startled myself by saying *yes* without ever thinking about what I had said. She asked me in a light manner to describe it and began to ask was it a chubby figure with short white wings and so on—you know, the pictures of them flying around and playing on harps and such. We all laughed and I excused myself, and they continued their chatting as I sauntered down the hall. My thoughts went to another place and time.

I haven't traveled all that much, but once I was in Italy on a hill overlooking Florence. As the sun was going down on a long day, there was a young female artist trying to capture the moment on canvas. When I told her how beautiful her painting was, she thanked me, but I could tell she was disappointed in her results and out of her frustration said, "There's so much more; there's something missing."

I traveled on to Rome, viewed the Sistine Chapel, and looked at all of the art, and she was right—there was something missing. We traveled to the Tivoli Gardens and there were artists everywhere, trying to capture the beauty all around them. Oh, the drawings were superb, no doubt, but the brush and oil were just not enough. I have read some good author's works, and it's difficult to draw a picture with a pen to make it believable. I was in the process of writing about some thoughts about my past and had already had some frustrations of trying to jot down my emotions and came to the conclusion it was impossible for me to convey much in any way of importance to the grandkids, but the thoughts about the angels kept bumping around in my head. Some of the angels have come and gone while others remained around me each day. Nothing had ever been written or told about them, so I would start again, trying to put down my thoughts and emotions about them.

It was late in the afternoon when we arrived at the small country home at the southern edge of Carlisle County. We had gotten there in a wagon drawn by Beck and Kate. The road was nothing more than a wide mud path. The time was early World War II—winter, I think it probably was. There had been the death of a relative. It was customary for friends and family to sit with the body until the undertaker came and prepared the body or took it to the funeral home. I don't recall ever going to or seeing any such funeral home at that time, but it was decided the body would remain at home. As the night fell, I wandered into the room and saw the outline of a small frail body at a slight angle, and a voice from a dark corner said, "That was my grandfather. He was my friend."

The voice sounded like a young girl but was in fact the voice of Andy, a young lad who had some birth defects. As he stepped out of the darkness into the light of the coal oil lamp, I saw him for the first time—something like out of the picture show *Deliverance,* although, looking back now, we all looked like the hill character. He was a very small, delicate being with sad eyes and a very weak body. He never said another word except, "He was so kind." All through the night, people would wander through to pay their respects as only country Southern people could do, and I kept hearing the words describing the old man and his kindness. We stayed all night and as I wandered through the old farmhouse, which consisted of three or four rooms at best, I noticed an old, empty rocker pulled close to the fireplace, and an old lady said it was his chair and that's where he read the Bible.

I wandered down the hall to Andy's room. As I think back, it was behind the kitchen, and you could feel the heat from the backside of the fireplace—the only source of warmth I could see or remember. There were no toys or things of a child, only a small dog lying at the foot of the bed. His name was General Lee, I was told, and the boy was named after Andrew Jackson.

The night dragged on, and more people arrived with the same haunting words about the old man's kindness. Even though I couldn't define the word, I knew its meaning. As the family left to go to the graveyard, my grandma and granddaddy and I stayed behind. I looked down the road at a hearse pulled by two black horses; black plumes garnished the harness. I had never seen a sight before or since like that. I walked back to the kitchen where Mama Mills was washing dishes. The table was full of food brought all through the night by friends. The aroma of the food blended with the smoke from fire in the fireplace being tended by Daddy Mills. It permeated the entire house, making the air heavy with all smells. We left before the family returned, and as I looked back at the old house as we left, I remembered looking at Andy's friend. Now after all these years, I know about losing family, but losing a friend is almost unbearable.

We returned in the late spring; the trees were full of leaves and the grass as green as emeralds. As we came up to the front door, Andy and the dog came out to meet me. He wasn't outwardly sad as before but all smiles, and he started asking questions about the outside world that I lived in. He was completely isolated; his parents were well beyond their years. "Would you like to see General Lee do some tricks for you?" I said yes and we walked and talked together 'til we reached the dirt road in front of the house. There wasn't any command—verbal or hand signal. The dog turned flips and ran in circles and Andy said, very childlike, "Do you like my dog?" I nodded in disbelief from watching General Lee. He said, "Do you see that tree down yonder? General Lee will bring you back a leaf." With that, the dog tore out down the road, leapt high in the air, got a leaf and was bringing it back when I felt Andy staring at me. I could barely make out his smiling face when the dog brought back the leaf. "Would you like to see him do it again?" he asked, and the dog again went out on his mission. But this time, I watched Andy. He was smiling the biggest smile you could imagine, but he saw me looking and said, "We don't want to tire General Lee too much, do we, Jerry?" "No, I guess not," I said. So we went back to the house where the adults were talking. Young people didn't speak too much in front of the older people back then, so we didn't say any more, but the dog was sitting in front of Andy staring at him and they seemed to be one.

 I saw Andy two or three other times in the summers, but I moved away. His parents died in the late 50s and early 60s. I saw my friend of my youth one last time, sitting on the steps of the old folks home in Arlington after I had graduated from graduate school. The home should have been called the home for the forgotten. I just couldn't bear going to see him, and I think he wouldn't have wanted to see me. All his friends were gone now. So I'll always remember him with General Lee, but his words remain with me to this day. "You know, he was my friend."

 Trying to describe him with words can only be

summed up by thinking of an iris with its soft petals strewn with dew in the early morning. Flowers and their smells are the only way to describe an angel. We have all seen and smelled them. So instead of trying to describe the angels I have seen, I'll just mention flowers we have all known.

We had just learned about our small Methodist church not being able to have the circuit rider coming once a month, and the building along with the old Springhill School would be scheduled to be torn down. It was late summer, and it was decided on by the small congregation to just sing some songs 'cause we didn't have a preacher. In the summertime, the windows were up, and the coal oil lamps sent their yellow glow over the small congregation. You could hear a lone whippoorwill singing its lonesome call through the night air. Along with the night sounds came the smell of honeysuckle. Sweet aroma filled the small church on the hill overlooking the cemetery of lost residents of the community. As all the people joined in the singing of the old songs, there came a feeling from inside the boy's soul like a spring at the back of their small farm. He quit singing and just read the lines of the songs quietly to himself. The spring began to spill over and tears ran down his face. That night in that old country church on the hill, he learned about kindness and what it would mean to be surrounded by angels for the rest of his life.

Uncle Lenny had two daughters. One was dying of kidney disease. She was small and so frail it was hard to believe she could be alive. When the boy came in to the room to visit, it was like the honeysuckle; she was so sweet and kind. Words can't do her justice, and only an iris can describe her. Her name was Mary Lee. The boy can still remember going into her room—more like a prison, I expect—and her face lighting up with her big smile and asking him questions, all about school and crops and about his life. Her kindness was not forgotten, and the spring flows when he thinks of her today.

Cousin Luther also had two daughters, Trevor and Ruth, both so kind, their voices soft like petals of a rose. They would talk to the boy in low tones only he could hear, with others sitting near. They would always make him feel special and warm. Although they have been gone for such a long time, he can still hear their soft murmurs in his ear. Irises with dew on their petals can only describe them.

As the boy grew to young adulthood, he heard fathers tell their young boys: *Don't cry; be a little man; don't show your tears.* But then he came to know a man named J.B. J.B. taught the boy it's okay to cry, and his kindness overshadowed all the other positive things he stood for. The boy tried to pattern his life after him but always came up short. He was his friend, but he died a while back only to become an iris in the garden. The boy also had a school friend named John. He, too, had this quality of kindness. He displayed this talent many times in their friendship through the years.

The garden with all the flowers the boy had known was growing—now at a rapid pace, as the boy reached manhood and eased on down the river. All gardens have a special place for special flowers. This is where all the mothers he had known down through the years live today. There was Rosemary, Alyce, Florida, Mama Gregory, Mama Burkhart, and Mama Mills. This is the place where the most special irises—pale lavender, almost white—grow. But gardens must be watered for dew to appear on the petals. This is when the spring overflows, when he remembers each special flower.

The next time someone casually mentions angels, I will say to myself: *You could have angels all around you if you learn how to water your garden.*

Whispers

It was a special time in the old man's life. The Lord had blessed him away above what he deserved. The time was September, Year '01, right after the terrorist attack in New York. The place was western Manitoba, Canada. He was duck and goose hunting with his son and six-year-old grandson. It was the magical time before night's end and the start of a new day. There was a light southern breeze blowing as they placed the last decoy in anticipation of some earl arrival geese. He lay down on the ground after setting all the decoys and looked up at the stars. The air was so clean it looked like you could reach out and touch them. Hearing a lonesome train whistle a way off in the distance and a lone C-47 freight plane laboring on its early morning run from Winnipeg to Regina, Saskatchewan. He reached down, took a loose handful of the prairie soil, felt its texture, and placed it close to his nose and smelled its aroma. His mind drifted back to a more gentle and forgiving time in his life.

The little boy ran to the pantry in the old farmhouse to wash and weigh some eggs with his grandmother. She had toled him off so his mom and dad could visit some friends in town. As he washed the eggs and placed them in the papier mâché mold, he turned to his grandmom and said, "They're gone." She said, "How do you know?" And the little boy of three smiled and went back to washing the eggs. There were many such times when he seemed to know more than he was supposed to.

Take the time his granddad couldn't find a lamb. The boy put on his sheepskin coat. He said, "I know where it is," and he led his granddad to where the lamb lay behind an old door behind the shed. There was also the time when his grandmom counted the baby chickens two or three times and came up with three missing. The boy walked to the place where they were—behind the old brooder box—and said to her, "They're here." But the time when the peddler man came and he was trading eggs for his grandmom's Christmas presents brought about some raised eyebrows on her part.

The old peddler wagon was just an old black pickup—with a homemade box with let-down sides—that was stained with chicken mess running down the sides. Several chicken coops graced the top and were full of old laying hens past their prime. As the door opened, the boy asked for six needles, one spool of thread, and one thimble. As the old peddler was reaching for each items and telling how many eggs it would cost, the boy had already reached into his little basket and taken out the correct number of eggs even before the old man could come up with the exact amount of eggs. This didn't go unnoticed by the old woman, and after the peddler left, she questioned the boy of six.

"How did you know how many eggs to put on the shell?"

He said, "I hear whispers."

She questioned him more about the lamb, chickens, and all the way back to when he was washing and weighing the eggs. He again said, "Just whispers," and smiled.

* * *

As he lay there on the ground, he began to think

about many of the things he held dear and had learned so many lessons from, the events and places from his childhood and about the whispers that had come to him before the leaves. He reviewed the lesson he had learned from his early childhood. *It was: Never doubt the ability of some children hearing voices or seeing things that adults can't hear or see. Never sell a child short.* As he lay there, he began to recall more of these old lessons that had become a part of him.

Isn't it kind of funny how people trace their lineage back to Ireland, Germany, and all the other countries and wind up with a long list of names with no faces or color, or nothing about who they were or what they did or their feelings. Well, I was hung on one of those limbs long ago, he thought, and even though many of the people he had written about may or may not be that close of kin, they were to him and deserved to be put in some kind of order. You may not be interested in this at all, but in years to come, you will know how they came to mold me into what little I am.

It's like a rose you would save from some occasion and place inside the pages of a favorite book or Bible only to look at it at some future date. When it was originally placed in between the pages, its color was brilliant and the petals soft to the touch, but after years of time passing, the rose's color, smell, and feel have changed and faded with time. Even the event has lost much of its endearment. The same thing happens with homes when the folks who lived there are gone. They turn into old broken-down monuments. The broken windows look like hollow eyes staring back at you. The worn bleached clapboard. Unkempt yard. Old flower beds needing care.

What made the whole show go was the people on that family tree and the branch in the time frame they lived.

They were the roses of their day, full of life, color, texture, and smell. You could feel their presence because their lives touched and molded you. Now they're all gone and, like the rose in the book, are fading with time only to be remembered by few and will soon be forgotten along with me. Lesson learned: *Each of us has a life, and life is short and death long—however, only if you watch the clock.*

Well, it's the Christmas of 1946. All Christmases are special, but this one was the boy's most memorable 'cause his mom and dad and Uncle Clarence were back home for Christmas. He and his granddad had cut a small cedar tree up around Springhill, a couple of miles from home where the sawmill stood. His mom and dad were stationed in Missouri during the war where his dad, a sailor, worked on war electronic equipment. His mom had also worked for the war effort in a jelly bomb factory. She may have been responsible for the deaths of many Germans. You may recall the burning of so many cities and factories in Germany on the war newsreels you got to see at the picture show back then. Clarence had been a paratrooper and jumped behind enemy lines during the Normandy invasion. But that was all behind us now, and the nation was beginning to heal from all the work and fears that go along with war-torn years.

The old farmhouse hadn't had electrical power very long so the little tree only had seven lights—one white, which went on top, two blues, two reds, one green, and one yellow. There was lots of hard candy, apples, and oranges, but money was scarce and presents few. It didn't matter; everybody was home for Christmas. Mama Mills had to have everybody visit all the kinfolk and neighbors. She was so proud of them and to have them home safe again.

She had cakes and pies and fried chicken with all the

trimmin's. The boy stood by, watching her ice a jam cake. When she finished, the cake must have weighed twenty pounds from all the juice she poured into it. He said, "Seems sort of funny . . . a little while ago it was just you and Daddy Mills here. Now there are twice as many people. Just seems funny, don't it?"

The boy watched the face of his grandma light up and with that funny little grin, she said, "Twice as good now."

New Year's came in the same old way—a stroll across the field to Uncle Clyde's and Imogene's to eat supper, which was roasted ducks and all the fixin's . . . and I mean fixin's; she was a great cook. Clyde had killed two big plump drakes and had brought them by to show the boy a couple of days before. When things froze up, there would be holes in the ice on the Obion where the ducks would roost and keep the water from freezing up. Clyde was a deadly shot. He had used his double-barreled Parker to kill supper. After everybody had eaten their fill, he would step out on the front porch, load his old Parker double barrel, and point it up in the sky and let fire. A big long orange glow would come out of the barrels and a roar would sound that would echo off of Cousin Luther's woods. That was the end of the fireworks 'cause everybody would be fast asleep when the New Year came in except for Mama Mills who would be darning socks or sewing at that late hour.

We would eat again at Clyde's and Imogene's house when a big fight was advertised. We would gather around the big radio and listen to Joe Louis, Jersey Joe Wolcott, and Marciano fights. It would be the talk of the neighborhood for weeks. Thinking back, I can almost hear the sounds and the announcer saying, "There's a jab and a right cross to the challenger by the champ."

Clyde was light years ahead of others around home

on raising cattle. He would take me to Charleston, MO to the cattle sales and would buy my dinner, but I can still remember the way he would say, " 'Bout time for some creme, don't you think?" And he would stop and buy me and him ice cream cones. Boy, it tasted good. Store-bought cream was always a big treat back then.

In the springtime, Clyde would carry the boy fishing up on Kentucky Lake to Cypress Creek. When the boy went off to college, he guided for Mr. Morgan, who had the only boat dock that would hire him to guide. He went to the same spots Clyde showed him years before, an he was known as a pretty good guide back then. He thought that Clyde must have seen the area before it was flooded 'cause the boy always caught a big mess of fish when he visited Clyde's old haunts. The lesson he learned from Clyde was: *It's not worth owning if you can't give it away.*

As his mind traveled back, he remembered walking into the old Springhill store and all the sights and smells of the spices and food and wood stove. There was the old post office section, the grocery store area, and the old back section with harnesses all over the wall and a few implements sitting around. A big wood stove sat in the middle of the room with the allotted characters of the community sitting, whittling, spitting, and spinning yarns. As the little boy strolled through that part of the store, one of the old men would always spin him a yarn and then laugh and go back to whittling. There would be a big pile of shavings that would start tomorrow's fire. The boy would study long and hard on these memories, trying to come up with a sound lesson, and one day out of the blue, it struck him: *What we do today has an effect on tomorrow.* Whispers was always there with the right ingredient—soft Southern breezes and quiet times free from worry and time on his hands.

Columbus Belmont Park was a favorite place in the boy's memories—family picnics, mostly summertime. But this last time—sometime around the third grade, just before he had to go to Louisville when his dad went to dental school—was the most special time. As the sun was setting, he wandered off to the bluff alone. He looked at all the trees around him, and he looked down below at the different trees next to the Mississippi River. He knew about the strong oak and hickory trees but not much of the lowly willow. He asked his granddad why they were different. "The oaks have to withstand storms and wind, but the willow has to withstand floods and storms and wind." What Lesson can be taught from this: *Life is full of storms, floods and winds. Be like the willow; bend but don't break.*

Some of his most favorite memories revolved around the Lampkin family. Cousin Luther's pappy rode with Forrest during the War of Northern Aggression. He would sit and tell the boy all about the raids and skirmishes that he remembered his pappy telling him when he was very young. Of course the tales were always slanted to the South, but that didn't matter; everyone he knew leaned that way anyways. He heard the same stories over and over until he knew what was going to be said before the words were spoken.

As the old man thinks back on these special times, he can almost put himself back on the porch with the night sounds and smells coming from inside of the old home, sifting through the screened door. The ladies of the house would always serve lemonade and sugar cookies and would ask if the boy liked Papa's stories. He would nod yes and say, "It's almost just like I was there."

They're all gone now and it seems like a long lost dream now caught up in a soft Southern breeze in his mind. He thinks to himself the lesson he learned was: *Even though the cause may be lost, never give up. No matter the cost, never give up.* Whispers would come to him late at night and they would reconstruct the events of the day and get them straight in his mind and it would be recorded in his mind to be brought back at some later date in *all* its entirety.

As the memories flash in front of his mind like an old newsreel, he thinks back in time to a small tent show that came to town generally in September. The little show's name was Bisbees Comedians. It consisted of a small troupe of actors—maybe ten—and one comedian. By today's standards, it would be quite a joke, but back then it was quite a show. In his mind he could still see Jim Brummel selling popcorn and snow cones; his pay was to get into the show. There was a small band made up mostly of the actors.

The play would start with the short introduction about what the three acts were going to be about. His all-time favorite was "Toby Goes to Town," Toby, being an old hayseed character, was so funny you could look at him and laugh. He didn't have to say anything to get laughs from the little country audience. The tent show would stay for a week, then move on to Bardwell and up to LaCenter. It's been said they played all the little towns up and down the Delta all the way to Marion, IL and Sikeston, MO. These late summer evenings were very special to him as he recalls all the colors, sounds, music and laughter. It saddens his heart that that way of life is gone, never to return. The lesson he learned: *Not all progress is progress.*

As he enters in his mind the little white church at Springhill, he recalls the stale smells and the echo sounds of the preacher talking to the small congregation. He would holler and rant for hours, it seemed. After church was over, his grandma would ask him, "Don't you feel better for going to church?" The lad would turn to the stoic face of his granddad and say, "No'm, he makes me feel bad." She would just smile as they rumbled down the dusty gravel road. Then once a month, they would go to the other church across the road. In spite of the preaching and in spite of his feelings, he learned a lesson that lasted a lifetime: *No matter what name is above the door, He lives in all churches.*

It was August 18th. The boy was fourteen years old. He had been hunting squirrels in the bottom for three days. It would be the last time to spend the night in the only home he really ever knew. The whispers were coming less and less now. As he listened to his favorite radio station, he would think to himself, *I wonder what it's like in New Orleans and Oqulegual, Mexico, and even Cincinnati, OH.* He was so tired he just lay back on the old bed that still had the old feather bed he used to sleep in when he was a little boy. As he lay there half asleep, tired and happy, Whispers spoke to him and in a soft voice said, *Start at the first thing you remember and record the events deep inside you.* As he lay there, his whole life went before him, day by day. He was amazed to see all those days in such detail. The colors, smells, voices had all been stored well and placed there for future review, he thought to himself, but Whispers said, *It's your gift.* His grandma came in to wake him to go hunting, but he hadn't really gone to sleep, so she left him to get a nap. When he got up, he began to tell her about past events.

She said, "How can you recall in such detail?"

"I guess it's a gift," he said and, smiling, went on off to the bottom. It was the last time he would hear from the Whispers for a long time. It was the last time he would ever sleep at home. Lesson: Time moves on, but when soft times come over your soul, think back on these times and cherish them.

While visiting his grandmother in the rest home, they talked about the past times, even before he was born, all about the people they had known. As he looked back at her when he reached the door to leave, she asked him, "Hear from Whispers lately?"

"No, ma'am, not for a long time."

"You will later on," she said, with a slight smile on her face. He could still remember that smile. His granddad had been gone nigh on twelve years then and nothing looked bright for her. *Now it's not so good, but it comes to us all,* he thought.

Suddenly, he was stirred and brought back in time by the sound of his grandson saying to his daddy, "I want to go tell Poppy something." As the little boy stumbled in the half light, knocking several decoys down in the process, he finally reached the old man. "Thanks for bringing me hunting in Canada with you. I love you, Poppy." As fast as it happened, he was gone.

There was a voice only he could hear that said, "Quite a ride, huh?"

Yes sir, quite a ride, he thought.

"Would you, if you could, change anything?"

He paused and said, "If I could just go back."

And the voice said, "You can and will. It's all recorded in your thoughts. Just reflect any time."

You know, there's nothing like hearing the voice of an old friend, he thought. She said he would return and he did. Welcome back, ol' friend. Welcome back, Whispers.

I think it's been said, "There are often subtle differences between greatness and mediocrity." Maybe not so subtle. It's however you spin the ball and look at things from different perspectives. I just hope my thoughts are somewhere in between. I am trying to say there's some good and bad in most generations. Before we move on, be sure we are throwing away the bad.

Coloil and Watkins Sav

On a recent deer hunt on my old home place, I was fortunate to observe a contrast. Few are left to know or care about the differences. There are some folk who might refer to this as a time warp. It is represented by those people who have lived long enough to remember things about the past—things that have been discarded as time moves along—but who also enjoy all the great advances of the day.

It was very cold and windy in late October. The ground was lightly frozen on top with a generous scattering of frost. The sunlight was dancing through the frost as if through a prism and, along with all the brightly colored sumac, all the colors we know were brightly displayed. The silence was broken as a new four-by-four truck slipped into the corn field. The driver stopped the truck next to an old decaying cross tie—the only remnant of an old fence line. He didn't know or care what that post represented to the old man who was watching from afar.

The door slowly opened, and a very young man eased out of the truck. He had his thermos in one hand and a couple of quart plastic containers in the other. As he approached one of the biggest green combines that's made today, he began to put the oil in the sleeping giant. He poured himself a cup of coffee, and soon the job was completed. He discarded the [oil] containers on the ground. Some time last April, he had called the gin in town and told them to deliver fertilizer, lime, and herbicide and spread them in a couple of applications. He came to the field a short time later with a sixteen-row Kinsey planter and planted the crop. Now he was back to harvest the crop in even less time than it took to put the crop in.

The young land tenant—for lack of a better term—sidles up to the door of the green giant and climbs inside the cab. He fumbles with dials for air control and flips on the Jim, Bob, and Billy radio program and turns on the key and instantly the machine belches out a black burst of smoke through the stack. It coughs a couple of times; a computer onboard adjusts the fuel flow, and then all he heard is a gentle hum.

He pushes the throttle forward and eases down rows of corn disappearing into the belly of the machine. All the remains of the shucks, cobs, and stalks come out the back in a cloud of dust. He lumbers on, and after a few rows, he reaches for his cell phone for the truck to come and offload his now full hopper of corn. He stops to enjoy another cup and turns the combine key off. He eases off in his new truck toward the subdivision where he lives. The old man who has been watching this event slowly walks over to where the empty oil jugs were left. He thinks back to when he would drain oil cans for at least a day, getting every last drop. He reaches down and pitches them in his poke. As he eases up to the piece of machinery, every so often there comes from somewhere a sigh followed by a low popping sound as the hydraulics relax deep from within the combine. This was the only thing that made one think it was more than a piece of steel.

Pretty effective, the old man thinks as he leans against the still-warm sleeping giant. He looks at the tracks it had left in the now-thawed ground. He sits down for a little while to rest and thinks back to the last time he was in the field and about the changes that have occurred. It was fifty-five years ago, he thought. His uncle had come over to his home and asked the boy and his granddaddy to help him gather corn the next day. "I would be much obliged if you all would bring your rig. You all can have a load," he said. "Be there," was all the old granddaddy said. No time or place was mentioned.

That night the boy laid out his clothes and draped his bibs and shirt and old Mackinaw jumper (which was his daddy's as a boy) over the back of a ladder-back chair. His little clodhoppers were placed next to his granddaddy's near the old wood stove so they would be sort of warm the next morning. When the boy went to the back porch to empty out, he looked at the sky. It was going to be one of the diamond crystal clear days, he could tell, *when the corn ears just fall off in your hand,* he thought, smiling to himself.

As they hooked up the team to the old rickety wagon the next morning—that magical time when it's not dark but not light yet—he eased off from the rig to take a lick at the salt block. It was pockmarked by many tongues that went deep into the block. It had become sort of a ritual with the boy now. If it was good for old Kate, it was good for him. Kate was his favorite mule.

The old man reaches down and picks up a dirt clod and some corn shucks and crushes them near to his nose. The smells of the past are very near now as he collects his thoughts about this field so long ago.

Back then, Uncle Clyde and Granddaddy started breaking ground in April at about the same time but on different sides of the fence. When all was plowed, they would disc, harrow, and plant. No fertilizer, no lime, no herbicide. Just Beck's and Kate's sweat. When the corn came up, it was plowed with a single mule and middle buster and then hoed until you got the plants up enough to shade out some of the weeds. That crop was a part of you and you were a part of it. Isn't it funny, he thinks, how when we think of the past, we really do see it from a rose-colored glass. That tenant will never know the smell of turned ground, the smell of honeysuckle, or the smells of corn shuck, while sitting inside a cab. What a shame, the old man thinks. When he was a boy, the weak spots were observed as they spent so much time in the field. They were mentally recorded and when the chicken house was cleaned out, it made its way to those areas. Always done by our hard work, he recalls with a slight grin. That crop was checked several times a week until it was made, which brings the old man back to that day so long ago.

  The team came to a stop at an old homemade panel gate that had rusty bailing wire on both ends to fasten to two tall straight black creosote railroad ties courtesy of the I.C.R.R. The brace posts were locust posts draped with its decaying bark that hung like a shroud in the dim light. The boy jumped down and undid the wire on one end to let the procession of Granddaddy's and Uncle Clyde's teams through. The ground was lightly frozen. The wind was from the northwest, and a cobalt blue sky was beginning to appear. His uncle and granddaddy spoke little and you had to be close 'cause they seldom repeated anything. "Remember snatch and pitch," his granddaddy said, referring to the corn ear with that funny little smile. Knowing all along he wouldn't be able to keep up. You see, he always got the down row. "What you can't get to the wagon, pile up. We'll come back and pick 'em up after a while."

  Even though they talked little that day, there was a never-ending chatter from the two old folks about things afoot in the little community—things like so and so bought that lot in the cemetery by the big persimmon tree or about what their wives had listened to over the party line on the telephone.

Sure enough try as he could, the boy couldn't keep up. He could barely hear the snapping of the stalks going under the wagon. It sounded like those firecrackers you could hold in your fingers—lady fingers their name. The vines, weeds, and stalks were taking a heavy toll on his legs. They looked beat up like blackjack saplins. But he knew that an old coal-oil-soaked corn cob and Watkins Sav would make all that hurt go away before supper time. The day wore on. They took the mules out of their trace to get a drink at the spring at the back of the place. As the mules, Granddaddy and boy drank from the same small pool, they took a moment to look at a train going by. "They'll be in New Orleans tonight," the granddaddy told the boy. There were as many as fifty trains a day sometimes back then. The smell of coal smoke, creosote, and the slough offered up a combined smell that could only come from that one spot in the whole world, he thought. As they went back to the wagon, his granddaddy saw blood on the boy's pants leg and said, "I got just the stuff to make it go away," and indeed he did.

When they left the field late that afternoon, the boy was pulling a string with a shuck tied, his dog jumping to catch the elusive prey. The boy said to his granddaddy, "I'll get the gate." It was the last time he would be back there until this day. The weight of the wagon and corn made deep marks into the now-thawed ground but even deeper ones into his mind. That night as his granddaddy dabbed on the coloil and gobs of Watkins Sav, he asked the boy what he learned. He studied a little while and said, "Them people will be in New Orleans now." His granddaddy smiled.

The old man raises himself on one knee and looks toward the Spring Slough and Trestle. *No more train,* he thinks. He looks at the track made by the rubber tire of the combine. *No more wagon ruts,* he thinks. He places his hand on the remaining broken-down cross tie post where the panel gate he closed long ago is now gone. He wonders what it will be like fifty-five years from now. He guesses both worlds are okay—each in their own time—but for that millionth of a second, he went back in time and heard his granddaddy say, "Daylight burning. Time to get the show on the road." Back at the barn, they once again watch the sun set and the boy slips off to take another lick of salt. The old man turns again to look at the setting sun and thinks what his granddaddy would say. One in a million. One in a million.

On his way home that night, he wonders. *As we (mankind) step forward, there is always one foot left in the past and only time will tell which is right.*

I bid you adieu,
Poppy

The Day the Preacher Came to Dinner

It's a cold fall night, and the old man pokes at the little fire in his fireplace. As the small bursts of sparks shoot up in a bright array of colors, he sees a lot of bright reds that remind him of colors of times upstream in his past.

It was a hot summer Sunday afternoon. His gramma had cooked food for two days, and he had helped her catch and kill three young pullets that morning to be fried for the preacher and his bunch. It was a big deal back then to have the preacher to dinner, and she had cautioned the boy and his granddad to be on their "P's and Q's." All the village was astir as to whose time it was for the preacher to come and seemed to be some sort of status symbol. The boy was just glad to see some other kids, even though their ages ranged from three to thirteen. He was ten years old, as he recollects, stirring the coals as he pitched another log on the fire.

They pulled up in an old black car with a broken spring on the passenger side due to Sister Fanny weighing three-hundred pounds. Blue smoke poured out from under somewhere. The tailpipe was wired with bailing wire to the rear bumper. When kids began to pile out windows and doors, they all had bright red hair. The girls had their hair done up in pig tails neatly tied at the ends with white cloth. They were braided so tight their faces looked like china dolls. The boys' hair was slicked down with a goose grease. They all had at least two-thousand freckles sprinkled all over their blue john colored faces. All their clothes must have been hand-me-downs 'cause they were all a size or two too small. Their britches were a couple of inches above their ragged socks. Their shoes were all worn out with holes in most of the soles.

Granddad and the boy brought out ladder-back chairs and put them under the old towering maple trees in the front yard. Gramma came out and asked if Sister Fanny would like to come back to the kitchen while she finished up with dinner, but she declined the invite—due to the heat, she said.

His granddad told the boy to sit down beside him and said to the boy, "I know this preacher is gassy, but he might say something you need to know." But after an hour of the preacher spouting of about ever'thing known to man with a whole bunch of yea's and thou's, the old man bent over and spoke in a soft voice, "You can go on. I was wrong. He doesn't know anything you or I can use, and I hope dinner's ready soon."

The boy rounded the corner where them red-headed children had disappeared some time ago only to find all his comic-book covers torn off and most of the wheels off his little cars gone. It was turning into one big disaster, he thought. About that time, his gramma hollered dinner time. At least he had some toys left as he ran and hid what was left.

That old table had so many vittles on it I swear it looked bent in the middle. The granddad asked the skinny little preacher to return thanks, and then he started in with all them yea's and thou's. About halfway through, the boy thought to himself, *What a wind jammer.* The preacher's kids sat at a second table where the boy and Gramma helped serve them. They were kicking each other under the table and pulling hair the whole time and making racket during the whole time food was being passed. Not one word came from the preacher or his wife to shut down some of the noise. They all ate like a pack of wolves, and the mound of food was disappearing. As the boy took his seat over in the corner, he pulled a small table up to him, tucked his napkin in his shirt, and waited patiently for some food to be passed his way.

He could see the big pile of chicken fast leaving the plate when his gramma said to the preacher's wife, "Sister Fanny, there's one piece of breast left. Don't get that gizzard or back." Something came over the boy, and he jumped up and spoke those unforgettable words, "Aw, shit far! It don't matter, Gramma. She's going to eat it all anyways." He didn't know the old woman could move that fast as she marched him to the back porch. He had never heard church bells ring before that day as his gramma began to put him some where in the middle of next week. The blows were quick and accurate. After the bells stopped ringing, he was sent out to the chicken yard to sulk 'til they finished dinner. He thought about how soft and white the preacher's hands were. "Soft as a lizard's belly," he uttered out loud, and his wife's fingers had fat bulging between the knuckles and joints. He knew neither one had probably worked a day in their lives, but he made a living saying all them "thee's and thou's," and about the Lamb on the tree.

He walked up to the cracked window in the corner of the kitchen to see the last sliver of two chess pies slide down Sister Fanny's gullet. All them kids came tearing out the back door at the same time, nearly tearing off the screen door. The big cotton ball that kept the flies away was flipped high in the air. Well, the boy's pony was infested with lice, and he and his granddad were going to put some medicine on her but hadn't gotten around to it yet, so the boy told the preacher's kids, "Ole' Dixie just loves for you to rub her, but mostly rub your heads up agin' her side." Shortly after they had all rubbed ole' Dixie.

The oldest boy pulled the porno-of-the-day—an 8-pager called *Popeye Rolls Olive Oil*. He came out with several words that the boy asked his gramma what they meant after a week or so and them bells rang again. So from all the encounters, the boy concluded they must not be so good. As dusk approached, they all piled into the old car and eased off towards home with all them red-headed kids scratching their heads. As the old granddad and the boy went toward the barn, the old man turned toward the boy and gently said, "Shit far, I'm glad that's over."

"Better watch them words, Granddad. Them bells can ring for you, too," said the boy. "Granddad, what about them gizzards?"

"Well," he said, "they go a long way 'cause the more you chew, the bigger they get."

The old man, looking far off and deep into the flames, smiles to himself and thinks about two sayings that stuck with him most of his life that explain how and why he is still suspicious about preachers. *How the twig is bent so groweth the tree.* And the other: *What you are speaks so loud I can't hear what you have to say.* He knows a couple of things for sure now that his river has many more and twisted currents than when the Master blew breath into him so many years ago. He will be there with Him when his river ends to carry him over to the other side.

I bid you farewell,
Poppy

The Baker's Dozen

The old man had finished setting out the last of his couple of dozen decoys and made his way in the dark to the little blind nestled between two small cypress trees. As he strained to pull himself into the blind, he, of all people, knew how much more difficult it was for him now to even put out decoys. To do simple things like getting in and out of the blind were becoming even more difficult for him now.

He had chosen to hunt alone today. This day, as the eastern glow began to explode into a rainbow of colors, ducks were on the move. He could hear their wings gliding through the cold morning air, even though it was still too dark to make out their forms or colors. He bent over slowly and carefully loaded his old 870 and set it aside. A brace of teal zipped through his stool of decoys and received only a smile from the old man. He was after bigger ducks—mallards. Then, there was a ripping sound of wings. *Close,* he thought, as the darkness gave way to the faint light. There was no wind, and their pinions made a tearing sound in the air in that magical time of day. The hen let out a blast of four-note sounds. The old man placed his call in his mouth and gave a response few could duplicate—a soft pleading call. The family of mallards turned, as if being pulled by an invisible string, and headed for the small opening between his decoys and the blind. For that magical moment, the old man and the ducks were one.

As his feathered visitors hung suspended over the decoys, the lead hen called again and again. The old fella' gave the softest of soft calls, and the ducks descended to the surface of the swamp with a gliding sound. The old hunter lowered his gun and gazed at the birds for that special time in his life, when he didn't have to bother killing to enjoy the moment. He noticed one small hen in particular, trying to call with her squeaky voice, and the funny, animated way she turned her head, trying to get the decoy to answer. Then, as swiftly as they came, they were gone.

Back at his decoy-making workbench, the old man reached for his last piece of cork and cedar and then started the last decoy he would ever make. He had completed a dozen decoys that week and used all of his material, except this one smaller-than-normal block. He had forgotten to send an order to the supplier on the East Coast, which generally took about a week for the turnaround time. *No matter,* he thought with a chuckle, *all I have is spare time now.*

The old man would come to his little shop at night and start a small fire in the tiny stove that sat off to one side. The smell of cork, cedar, paint, lacquers, and wood smoke filled his nose. *Great smell,* he said to himself. He talked out loud to himself a lot now. Not that many people came around to visit anymore.

He was about to place the head of the decoy on the cork body when his son came by to chat and have a cup of chocolate. The boy noticed the petite Susie but said nothing. As the old man placed the head, then the keel, the boy said, "Well, I'll see you tomorrow, and thanks for the dozen decoys," and he stepped out the door.

The old man began to get all his paints together, and, like the rest he had painted down through the years, he chose muted earth tones. They were similar to the colors he had seen on a cold, slate-tinted day. All his colors were selected from the pallet of different shades of old duck-hunting memories. They were different from the commercial colors on plastic decoys that stand out. His blended with the surroundings. Even though rain and snow would be on them at times, he decoys would always appear to be dry and not be shiny. He was proud of that fact because it would set him apart from the commercial decoy-makers. After the final paints were applied and dried, the old fellow decided to carve on the bottom of the small decoy a saying he had modified to suit his fancy from an old Chevy ad. After all, he did this one for himself. He said the words out loud as he etched them on the bottom and smiled after he was done.

He thought that no one would probably want this block, being it was small and the head cocked at a funny angle, like the little Susie that he remembered. *I'll just stick it back here,* he thought, as he placed it under a bunch of old pieces of cork wood. He went out to the rocker, sat down, put another stick of wood on the fire, and poured himself another cup of chocolate. He was stirring around, trying to find some marshmallows, when he felt something let go deep inside. He thought, *No matter, it's like a bunch of cows nudging up against a gate 'til it finally comes open, and the cattle wander into the new pasture while the farmer is watching and finally says, "Ah, shit, I was going to let 'em in next week anyway"* . . . this meaning the old fellow had seen and done about all he had ever wanted to and there wasn't much else to look forward to.

As he sat there thinking of duck hunts of the past, he recalled the baker's dozen, that morning as the ducks slipped into his small set-up. He remembered their voices, the smells and sounds of the swamp, as they glided into the water. The old man's carving knife slipped from his hand as he eased out into the heavens.

He had been gone quite a while before the young man could make himself visit the old shop. As he entered, he soon discovered others didn't feel as he felt and had ransacked the building, taking what they wanted. Search as he might, the young man couldn't find the last decoy. *It takes a special dude to steal, but to steal family treasures is the worst of all,* he thought.

Time moves on, and the young man starts his new life without the old man. Soon he has sons of his own, and he shares all the old stories of his dad and their hunts together. The old carver had given his last dozen decoys to him just before he died. The young man treasured them so much he placed all of them on his mantel, above the fireplace.

As time continued to march on, the young man had grown older and his sons were now out on their own. The man was traveling down through the southern part of Tennessee. He had taken quite an interest in antiques. He spied an old flea market and stopped to browse around. He sauntered up and down the aisles, viewing what was junk for some and treasure for others. All of a sudden, he saw what appeared to be the bill of a duck decoy. He pulled it out and began to dust it off and then this "feeling" came over him.

"Hey, lady, how much?" he asked.

She replied, "Oh, about a Yankee dime."

"How about a hundred?" he asked with a big smile.

"Sold!" she said.

You all know the feeling you get when you find something of value to you but which holds none for someone else? That was the most special thing that had happened to the man in a long time. That old decoy represented the final chapter that had been lost for some twenty-odd years. He washed and cleaned that old battered piece of cork and wood, then placed it on the mantel, next to the other twelve decoys.

Around Christmas, his boys were home, and the dad had not said a word about the "find." When one of the boys asked, "How come you have that old piece of junk next to Poppy's decoys?" The man picked up the old decoy, turned it over, and read the carved words, "There is a place that I know, that's far, far away and way, way afar, where only I can go, signed Poppy."

"Now you know," he said. They all smiled and began to tell stories of old duck hunts of long ago, where only they could go (memories). The Baker's Dozen were once again united.

In another dimension, somewhere in the heavens, there really is a place that is far, far away and way, way afar, where the old wood carver eases over to start warming some chocolate. He smiles to himself and says with anticipation in his voice, "The boys will be here directly."

I bid you farewell,
Poppy